DOUGLAS XTB2D-1 SKYP...

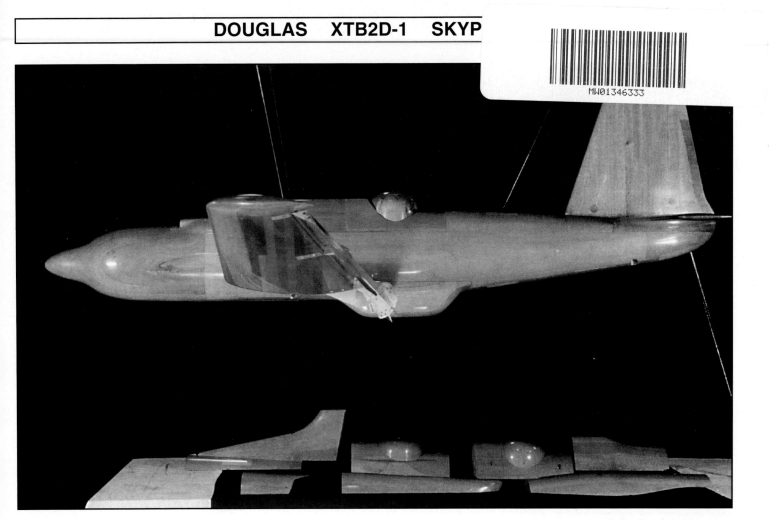

Above, wood wind tunnel model of the original XTB2D-1 concept on 2-20-43. Wood pieces for alternate configurations, including deletion of turret and gondola, are displayed beneath the model. The proposed flaps and flaperons are in the full down position.

Steve Ginter, 1754 Warfield Cir., Simi Valley, California, 93063

All rights reserved. No part of this publication may be reproduced, stored in a retrieval system, or transmitted in any form by any means electronic, mechanical or otherwise without the written permission of the publisher.

© 1996 Steve Ginter

INTRODUCTION

Bob Kowalski continues the saga of the Bomber Torpedo (BT) program and the similar Scout Bomber (SB) program with the obscure story of the Douglas XTB2D-1 "SkyPirate". The story started in Naval Fighters Number Twenty-Four, Martin AM-1/-1Q Mauler and continued with Naval Fighters Number Thirty, Douglas XSB2D-1 and BTD-1 "Destroyer". It is our intention to cover the Kaiser-Fleetwings XBTK-1 and Curtis-Wright XBTC-2 and XBT2C-1.

This book would not have been possible without the generous support of Harry Gann and Douglas Aircraft Division from which all material for this book was obtained unless noted.

This history is based on information contained in the 1943 "Detail Specification for Model XTB2D-1 Airplane Class VTB (three-place monoplane)", "Description, Dimensions and Leading Particulars", "Analysis of the Tactical Usefulness of the Model XTB2D-1 Airplane" dated December 1944, and from various XTB2D-1 airplane system drawings. The statements enclosed by quotation marks were taken either from those sources or relevant Pilot's Handbooks. Terms used in the story are terms used at the time the XTB2D-1 was built. These terms may have subsequently undergone refinement, for example the term "heat" instead of the "thermal" anti-icing system.

Anyone having photos or other information on this, or any other naval or marine aircraft, may submit them for possible inclusion in future issues. Any material submitted will become the property of NAVAL FIGHTERS unless prior arrangement is made. Individuals are responsible for security clearance of any material before submission.

ISBN 0-942612-36-1

BACKGROUND

In October 1943, the Navy ordered two prototypes of a long range torpedo bomber capable of operating from Essex class carriers and designated the XTB2D-1. The XTB2D-1 would carry a multiple tor-

ORIGINAL LONG-RANGE TORPEDO BOMBER STUDY (PRE-XTB2D-1)

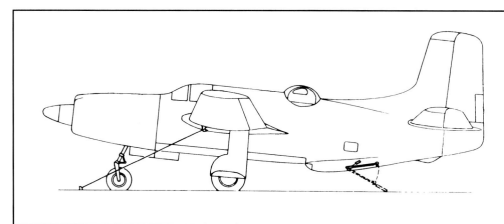

ARRESTING HOOK AND CATAPULT ARRANGEMENT

THE PRE-XTB2D-1 TAILHOOK RETRACTED INTO THE BELLY GONDOLA, WHEREAS THE XTB2D-1 DESIGN USED AN EXTERNALLY MOUNTED HOOK DESIGN.

DIVE FLAPS

THE PRE-XTB2D-1 DESIGN CALLED FOR THE SAME FLAP SYSTEM TRIED ON THE ORIGINAL XSB2D-1 DESTROYER. THE XTB2D-1 USED THE UNIQUE ROLLER FLAP / FLAP-ERON DESIGN.

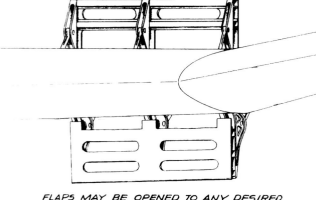

FLAPS MAY BE OPENED TO ANY DESIRED POSITION UP TO 90°

SECTION THRU WING AT DIVE FLAPS

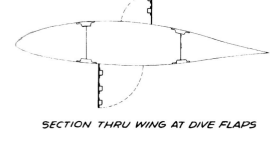

DIVE FLAPS

ARRESTING HOOK

SNUBBER AND RETRACTING CYLINDER

CATAPULT HOLDBACK HOOK

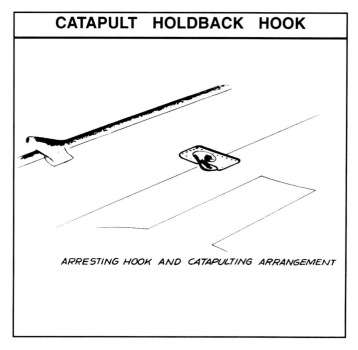

ARRESTING HOOK AND CATAPULTING ARRANGEMENT

ORIGINAL ARMAMENT PROPOSAL

TWIN-GUN TURRET

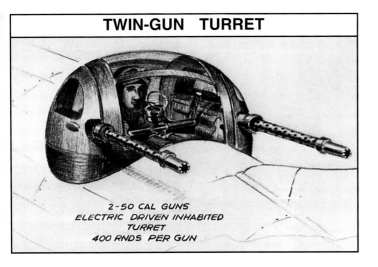

2-50 CAL GUNS
ELECTRIC DRIVEN INHABITED TURRET
400 RNDS PER GUN

THE PRE-XTB2D-1 STUDY INCORPORATED A TWIN-GUN TURRET AND REAR FIRING GONDOLA GUN. THE DIFFERENCE WAS THAT IN THIS ORIGINAL PROPOSAL A HAND HELD GONDOLA GUN WAS PLACED IN THE EXTREME LOWER TAIL, AS OPPOSED TO THE MID-REAR FUSELAGE MOUNTED REMOTE OPERATED GUN IN THE FINAL XTB2D-1 DESIGN. TWO WING GUNS WERE ORIGINALLY PROPOSED WITH THE FINAL XTB2D-1 DESIGN CALLING FOR FOUR. ANOTHER NOTABLE DIFFERENCE WAS THAT THIS PRE-XTB2D-1 PROPOSAL CALLED FOR A BOMB BAY AND INTERNAL BOMB LOAD ONLY INSTEAD OF THE EXTERNAL BOMB LOAD CARRIED BY THE XTB2D-1.

FLEXIBLE TAIL GUN

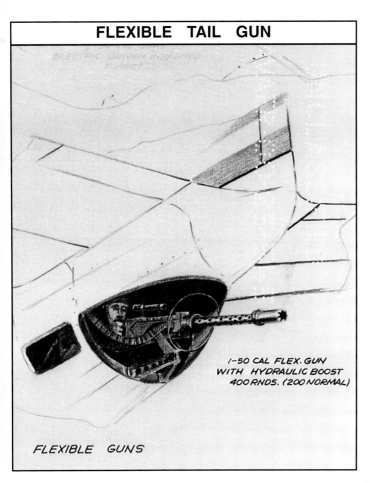

1-50 CAL FLEX. GUN
WITH HYDRAULIC BOOST
400 RNDS. (200 NORMAL)

FLEXIBLE GUNS

INTERNAL BOMB BAY

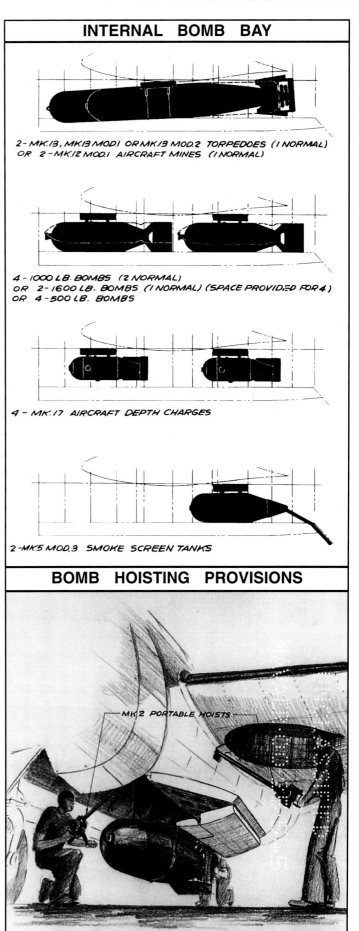

2-MK.13, MK.13 MOD.1 OR MK.13 MOD.2 TORPEDOES (1 NORMAL)
OR 2-MK.12 MOD.1 AIRCRAFT MINES (1 NORMAL)

4-1000 LB. BOMBS (2 NORMAL)
OR 2-1600 LB. BOMBS (1 NORMAL) (SPACE PROVIDED FOR 4)
OR 4-500 LB. BOMBS

4-MK.17 AIRCRAFT DEPTH CHARGES

2-MK.5 MOD.3 SMOKE SCREEN TANKS

BOMB HOISTING PROVISIONS

MK.2 PORTABLE HOISTS

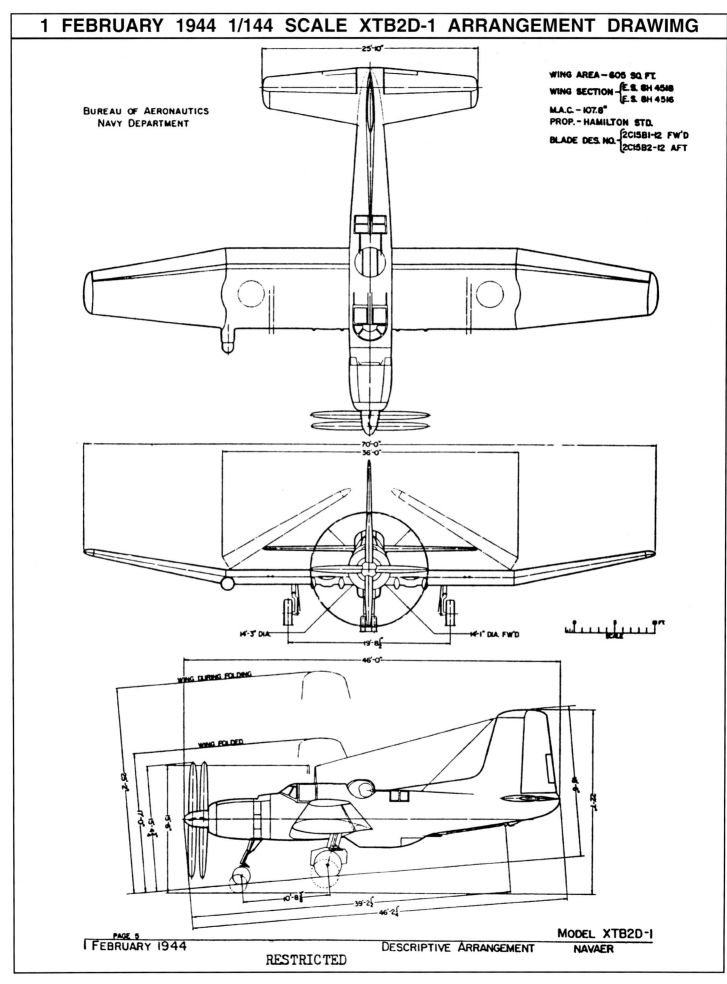

XTB2D-1 SKYPIRATE CUTAWAY

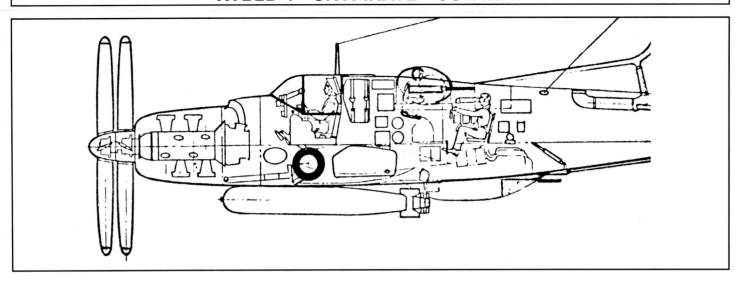

pedo or bomb load further and faster then the current torpedo bombers or those under development for the fleet. In any future battle with the Japanese fleet, that long range capability would have offered the US Task Force Commander the opportunity to launch his strike (TB2Ds, perhaps escorted by the long-ranged Boeing F8Bs also under development) well before the Japanese Task Force could launch theirs. With the subsequent US Navy victories in the sea-battles of 1944, the Japanese carrier fleet no longer was a factor to be reckoned with and therefore there was less need for the XTB2D-1.

Navy specifications required that

Above, short-tail mock-up. (Wayne Morris) Below, tall-tail mock-up on 9-20-44 with the two XTB2D-1s under construction in the background next to BTDs.

the XTB2D-1 be a single-engine, three-place landplane suitable for use as a torpedo plane, scout or, as if in a return to pre-World War Two thinking, a horizontal bomber. Other requirements included the use of the most powerful engine available, the Pratt & Whitney R-4360 Wasp Major, coupled to a Hamilton Standard counter-rotating propeller. The XTB2D-1 was designed around a full-span flap system that served to meet both the slow-speed and long range requirements, and also replace the conventional ailerons, landing flaps, and dive brakes. The ordnance loads were carried on four wing-mounted bomb racks, while the armament consisted of seven .50-caliber machine guns. The specified internal fuel capacity of 774 gals. could be supplemented by the use of 300 gal. droppable tanks. The fuel, oil and hydraulic systems were all required to function throughout a normal operating attitude range of 20° nose-up to 50° nose-down. The

The heaviest structural fuselage components were the cockpit stiffeners and keel rails that extended the entire length of the fuselage. The two cockpit stiffeners were used to support the weight of the cockpit sliding enclosures, the oil tank cover, the turret and bomber's compartment enclosures. The two keel rails were composed of three segments: the forward and aft rails were integral parts of the fuselage while the center rail was attached to the underside of the wing. The keel rails also supported the gun tunnel.

HORIZONTAL STABILIZER

For strength, the wing and horizontal stabilizer utilized hat shaped stiffeners spaced at five inch intervals on center between the spars, as illustrated at right on the photo of the horizontal stabilizer.

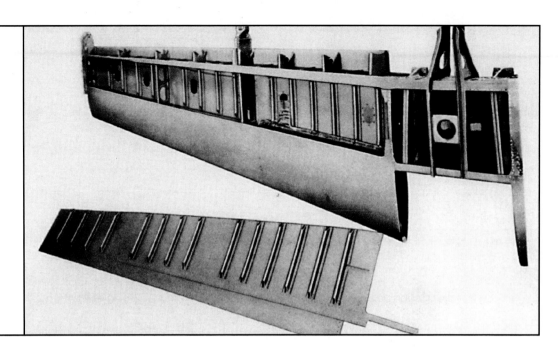

XTB2D-1 made use of both a tricycle-type landing gear and a horizontal stabilizer incidence-change device to improve its carrier suitability.

For its construction, the designers utilized the strength-carrying capabilities of the new alloys of the time in a stressed-skin system that would minimize drag and save weight. Because of this stressed-skin system, the fuselage no longer used conventional longitudinal stringers, relying instead on fuselage frames and circumferential stiffeners for rigidity. The heaviest structural fuselage components were the cockpit stiffeners and keel rails that extended the entire length of the fuselage. The two cockpit stiffeners supported the weight of the cockpit sliding enclosures, oil tank cover, upper turret and bomber's compartment enclosures. The two keel rails were composed of three segments: the forward and aft rails were integral parts of the fuselage while the center rail was attached to the underside of the wing. After being bolted together, the keel rails supported the weight of the gun tunnel.

The wing was a two spar structure constructed in three sections of a center wing panel and two outer wing panels, two wing tips and an auxiliary

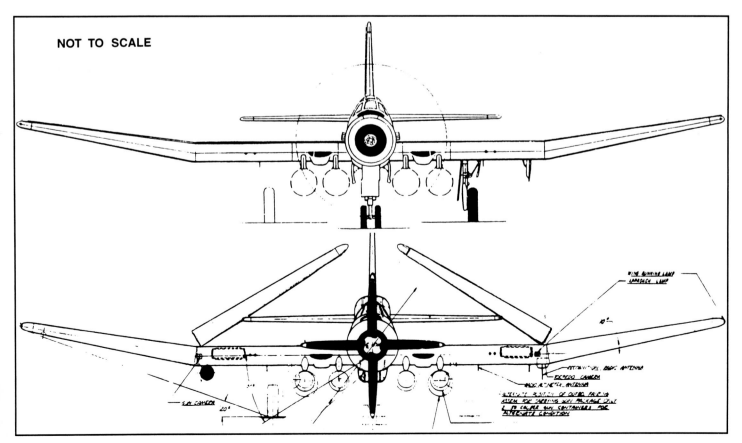

spar installed between the main spars in the landing gear wells. For its strength, the center wing panel used "closely spaced chord-wise stringers" to reduce "plating deflection from loads produced by compression" while its bending loads were carried by the spars. The outer wing panels, as well as the horizontal and vertical stabilizers, were similarly strengthened by using "hat shaped stiffeners spaced at five inches on center".

For its airfoil, the wing used a NACA laminar flow type that was modified to reduce pitching moment, decrease total weight of the wing structure, and increase its fuel-carrying capacity. In response to the airfoil's laminar flow requirement for a smooth surface, a heat anti-icing system was specified for the outer wing panels and tail surfaces. The outer wing panels incorporated a change of

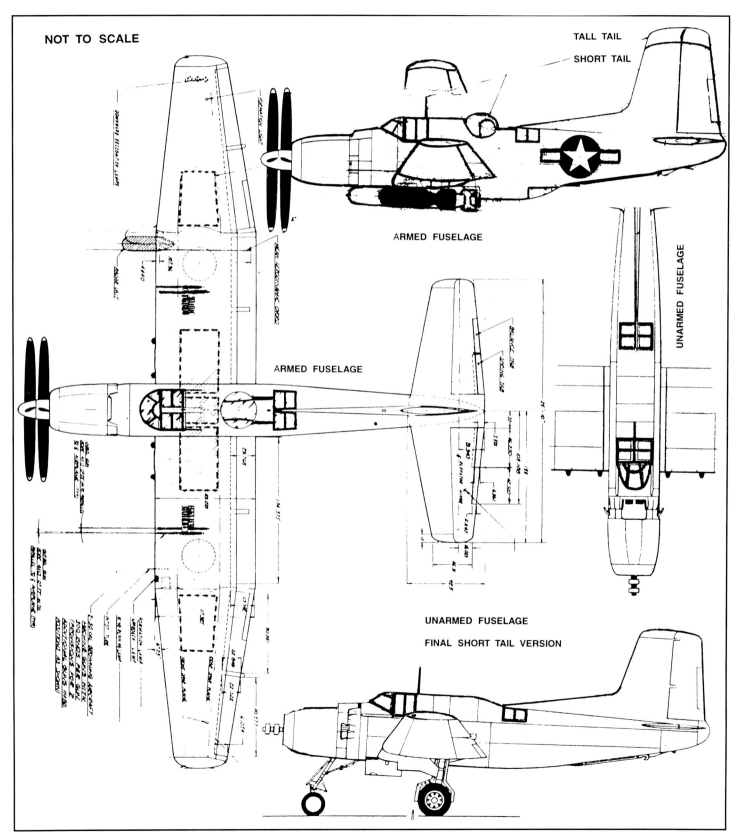

incidence, from +2° at their joint with the center wing to 0° at their tip. This "washout" or "twist", the resulting decrease in the angle of attack, was incorporated to overcome any tendency of the wing tip to stall.

An attempt at reducing the time needed to perform maintenance was made by the strategic location of the airplane's equipment to allow for quick access and simultaneous servicing. The specifications had also required that "access doors to equipment requiring frequent inspection or removal shall be located on preferably the right side of the fuselage". As an example of what this concept promised, the navy's goal for an engine change, to be accomplished by a work crew of four men, was one hour. That one hour goal included the time needed to rig the work stands, obtain access to, remove and replace

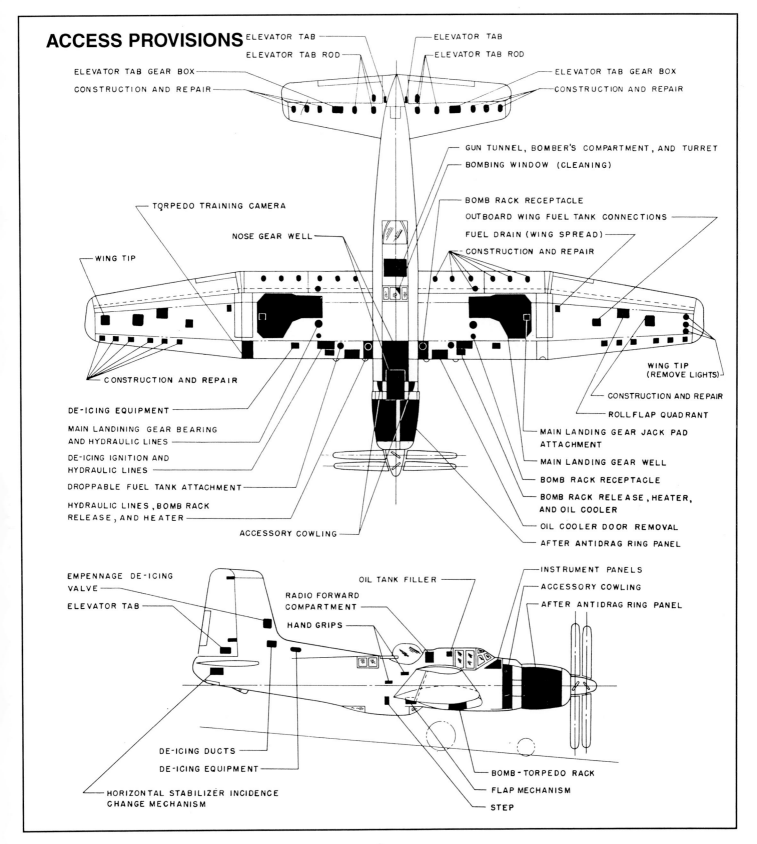

the unit, and close any openings used for access.

The airplane's electrical and hydraulic systems were the standard of the day. Its primary electrical system was a twenty-four volt, direct-current system composed of one engine-driven generator and two batteries. The airplanes hydraulic system was a 3,000 psi system that normally powered the operation of the landing gear, the main gear doors and brakes, the wing flaps and folding mechanisms, the dive brakes, and the arresting hook snubber and retraction. Its components included an engine-driven pump, a hand pump for emergency extension of the nose gear and emergency retraction of the dive brakes and landing flaps, and an air bottle for emergency brakes.

The Pratt & Whitney Wasp Major R-4360-8 featured a single-stage, variable-speed supercharger that was semi-automatic in operation, thereby offering a reduction in the pilot's workload. As usual, the pilot's primary control of the engine was his throttle, which now was connected to a manifold pressure regulator. The manifold pressure regulator operated the carburetor throttle to set MAP (Manifold Absolute Pressure), and controlled the speed of the variable speed supercharger. In order to maintain operating limits and provide stable operation, an intentional lag was incorporated into the engine's responses to throttle movement. This lag, known as "droop", occurred during the supercharger's variable speed range and was most pronounced at combinations of higher RPMs and higher altitudes.

The Navy normally assigned the design of the exhaust collector system to the airframe contractor, which helps explain why an engine would be equipped with different exhaust systems when installed in different airplanes. The R-4360's 28 cylinders were arranged in four radial rows (cylinder rows A, B, C, and D) of seven cylinders to a row with the similarly-located cylinders of each row being termed a "bank". The Douglas design combined the exhaust ports of two cylinders from alternate rows (A and C and B and D) of the same bank, into a "Siamese" (as in twins)

Below, the huge cowling doors are held open for servicing by a steel brace, and the metal service platform has been installed between the wing and engine cowl ring.

stack assembly. This coupling of exhaust ports reduced the effect of back pressure on the engine, thereby increasing its power. The "fish-tail" shape at the after end of each stack assembly was incorporated to act as a flame damper.

The high power output of the R-4360 demanded a propeller that possessed an area large enough to convert the powerplant's shaft horsepower into propulsive horsepower (thrust). The eight blades of the Hamilton Standard Super Hydromatic co-axial propeller had the necessary area, while the counter-rotation of its two sections served to eliminate torque. As in normal practice, the propeller pitch control was located on the throttle quadrant between the throttle and the mixture control. Because of the propellers' two sections, another set of controls was located on the left fuselage sidewall. These were labeled "FEATHERING, UNFEATHERING" and "PITCH LOCK", and would be used to control problems with either propeller section. As a short explanation of these safety features; "FEATHERING" would streamline a section's propellers in high pitch, stopping its rotation and minimizing drag, while "PITCH LOCK" was used to prevent a propeller from going into low (flat) pitch, as would happen if governor oil pressure was lost. The danger of flat pitch operation was that the resulting RPMs were high enough to create airplane control problems because of the excessive drag of the propeller section, and/or lead to ultimate catastrophic failure of the engine's reduction gearing.

The two sections of this propeller were of different diameters: the forward section was 14 ft. 1 in., while the after section had a diameter of 14 ft. 3 in. Although Hamilton Standard did response to my request for information about this difference, they were unable to provide any reasons for it. Reason would dictate that the difference in diameter was to improve the efficiency of the after section by extending its tips into the undisturbed air that existed beyond the vortices created by the forward section's propeller tips (these vortices formed

under certain atmospheric conditions as seen in some of the more notable photographs of World War Two deck-launches).

A tricycle-type landing gear was used because of these inherent benefits: it minimized ground looping, "the arresting hook could be placed

Above, head-on view of massive Hamilton Standard counter-rotating propellers minus the prop spinner. Auxiliary fuel tanks are fitted on the outboard wing store stations (XTB2D-1, #933 on 6-13-45). Below, close-up view of the seldom seen prop spinner. The spinner was blue and by 1945 the forward engine cowl ring was red. (XTB2D-1, #933 on 5-26-45).

XTB2D-1   NOSE   GEAR

well forward on the fuselage to decrease the landing space required", it facilitated ground handling, and prevented tail rise during engine runup. The main landing gear was mounted in the center section of the wing and retracted outboard into wells located between the two spars. The nose gear was mounted to the bottom of the engine mount and retracted into a well that extended aft to the forward wing spar. Its tail skid was designed to be free of projections, fittings or re-entrant angles that might engage the arresting wires, and provided to protect the after portion of the fuselage in the event of a tail low landing.

In operation, the landing gear was vintage-Douglas, simple and reliable. The gear lever was connected to the hydraulic selector valve operating all gear simultaneously, and to the up-latch release cable for each gear. Normal operation was hydraulic, with all gear being held up by positive, mechanical up-latches. In case of hydraulic failure, placing the landing lever to "DOWN" released the mechanical up-latches (the same as in normal operation), and the force of gravity would extend the main gear while the nose gear could be lowered by the hydraulic hand pump, using either any remaining system fluid or fluid that was intentionally trapped in its up-line. Then, as in normal operation, the mains were locked down by bungee springs bearing against over-center stops while a mechanical down-latch locked

XTB2D-1 NOSE GEAR

NOSE GEAR UP-LATCH

the nose gear down. This simplified description is included to show an early use of the landing gear system that epitomizes the design philosophy that has been a hallmark of Douglas airplanes.

The nose gear was provided with full castering capability, to aid in ground maneuvering, and a shock-absorbing strut that compressed during its retraction. Although the propellers' reduced diameter had allowed for a shorter nose gear strut, the length required to provide the specified 12 inches of ground clearance, was still too long to allow for the strut's retraction into the space available. The solution was a nose gear telescoping mechanism that consisted of a barrel and piston assembly that was attached to the right-hand side of the nose gear strut. During retraction, hydraulic pressure in the nose wheel actuating cylinder acted on the piston and compressed the strut for stowage in the wheel well. When the landing gear was extended, the weight of the nose wheels helped pull the oleo strut to its full length.

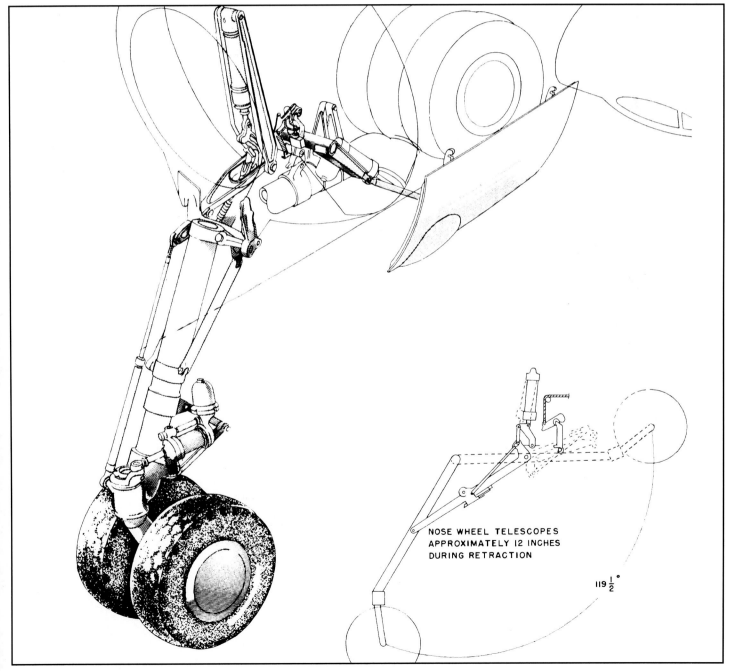

NOSE WHEEL TELESCOPES APPROXIMATELY 12 INCHES DURING RETRACTION

$119\frac{1}{2}°$

NOSE GEAR RETRACTING MECHANISM

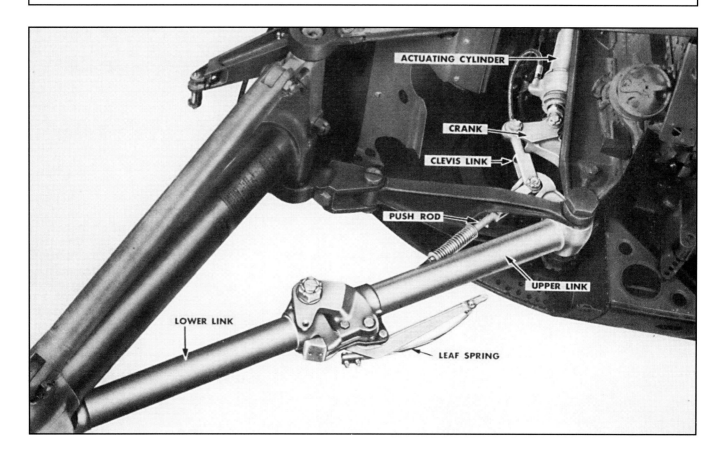

NOSE GEAR DOOR ACTUATING MECHANISM

XTB2D-1 ARRESTING HOOK

XTB2D-1 CATAPULT TOWING HOOKS

XTB2D-1 MAIN LANDING GEAR

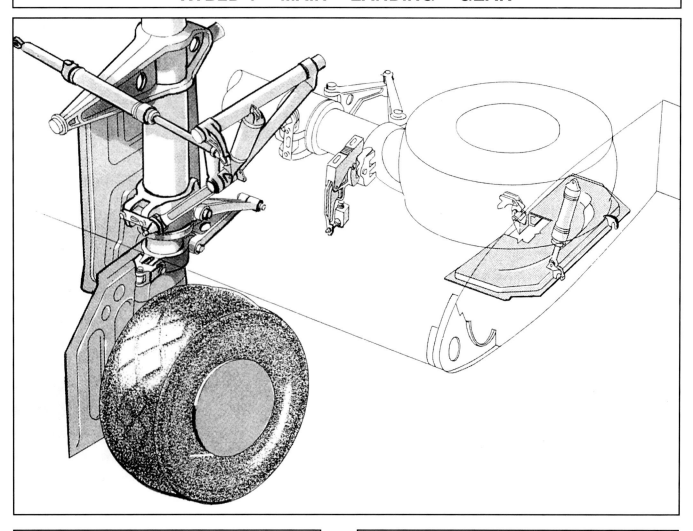

GEAR DOOR ACTUATING CYL.

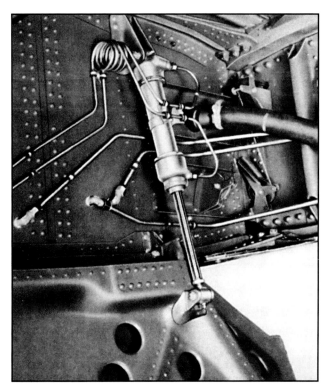

MAIN GEAR UP-LATCH

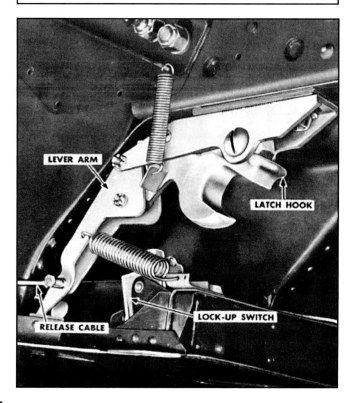

XTB2D-1 MAIN GEAR

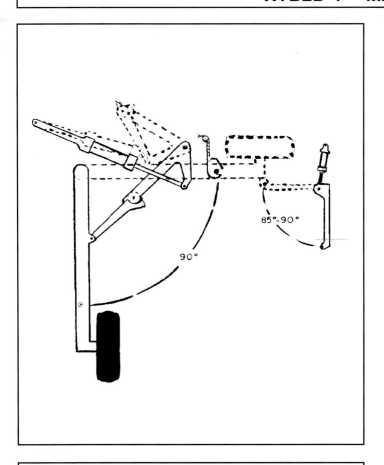

RETRACTING MECHANISM

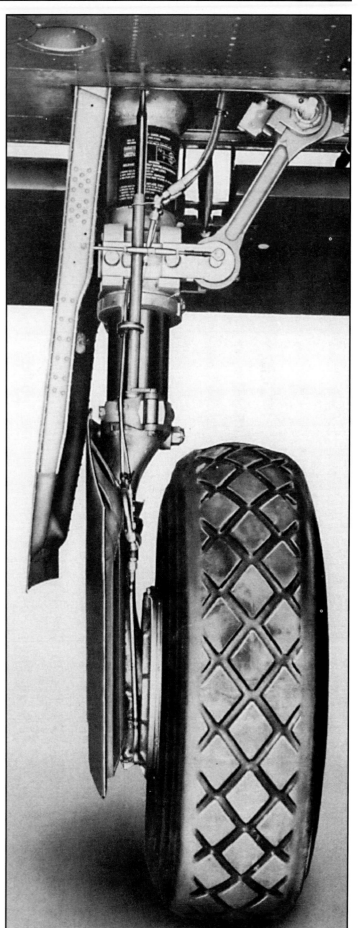

XTB2D-1 WING FOLD

UPPER RIGHT INNNER WING JOINT

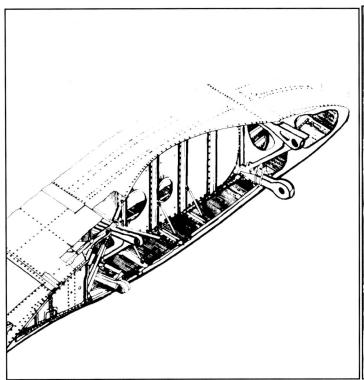

WARNING FLAG MECHANISM

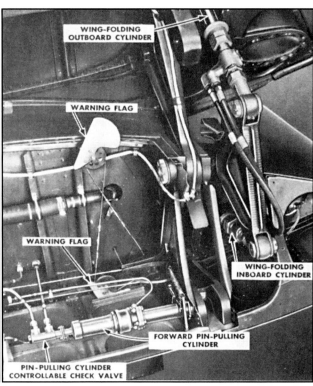

WING LOCKING MECHANISM AND PIN-PULLING CYLINDERS

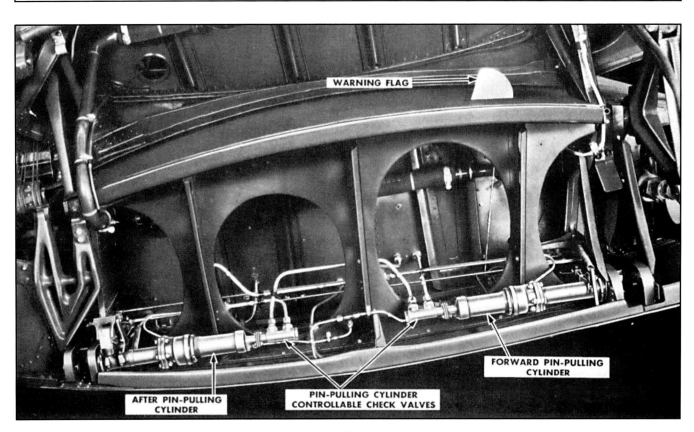

XTB2D-1 FUEL SYSTEM

The fuel capacity of the XTB2D-1 consisted of 774 gallons carried internally plus externally-carried, 300 gallon droppable tanks. The internal fuel was carried in non-metallic, self-sealing tanks located in the center and outer sections of the wing and mounted between the front and rear wing spars. The main fuel tank consisted of three interconnected fuel tanks (left-hand, center, and right-hand), located in the center wing panel with a total capacity of 501 gallons. The outboard wing panel fuel tanks were the "auxiliary wing tanks" and had a capacity of 136.5 gallons each. The filler fitting for the auxiliary wing tanks was located on the upper wing surface at the outboard end of the tank, and therefore these fuel tanks were capable of being filled when the wings were folded. The droppable tanks were constructed of several layers of nonself-sealing plywood material with a 300 gallon capacity.

An air-cooled engine has a trait of higher oil consumption then other types of engines. These "big" radials burned oil to the extent that, to help satisfy its long range requirement, the XTB2D-1 was equipped with a 60 **gallon** oil tank. The oil quantity carried for a given flight was varied according to the fuel load. In summary, the oil quantity would be 18 gallons when the airplane's fuel load was 302 gallons, 28 gallons when the main fuel tank was filled, 43 gallons when full internal fuel was loaded and 60 gallons when one or more droppable fuel tanks were part of the total fuel load. In all cases, this oil quantity was in addition to the 12.5 gallons of oil trapped in the system.

The oil tank was a self-sealing type, located in a compartment in the upper portion of the fuselage, aft of the pilot's rear armor plate. The oil tank compartment was attached to the cockpit stiffeners and designed so as to allow the oil tank to be replaced by two men in a specified time of one hour.

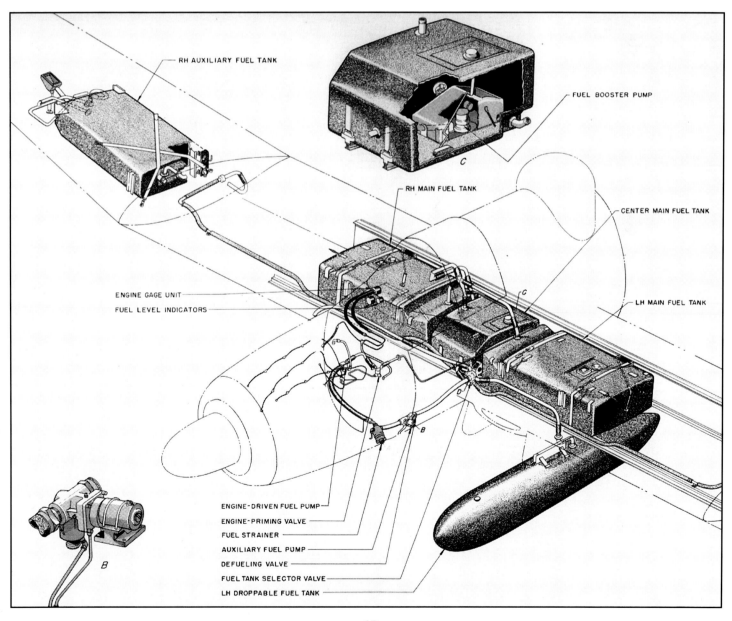

XTB2D-1   36933   ROLLOUT

Above, the El Segundo XTB2D-1 project crew pose in front of their aircraft on rollout day. Below, head-on view of 36933 on 2-18-45. When the wings were folded, metal braces were inserted between the wing center section and outer section for safety and stability. At right top, note wing fold, tailhook and tall vertical fin. The cowl ring is painted red. At right bottom, the aircraft is shown here spinnerless as it appeared throughout most of the Skypirates career.

ARMAMENT

To carry its ordnance, the XTB2D-1 was equipped with four Mark 51 Mod 7 bomb racks that were mounted under the center wing at wing stations 40 and 80, and streamlined by fairings that also enclosed the sway braces. Each of these bomb racks could carry any of the specified ordnance: torpedoes, 500 lb. to 2,000 lb. bombs, mines, depth bombs, or incendiary bomb clusters. Optional racks could be mounted at wing station 95.5, where structural limitations precluded the carriage of torpedoes. The normal practice was for the inboards (wing station 40) to carry the bombs or torpedoes while the outboard (wing station 80) bomb racks would carry the droppable fuel tanks. The APS-4 radar would be mounted under the starboard wing near wing station 206, and if used as a target-towing airplane, the tow target container would be attached to the left-hand inboard bomb rack.

As a means of improving its bombing accuracy, the XTB2D-1 was designed to be "flown" by its Sperry autopilot during the horizontal bombing attack. To accomplish this task, a greater degree of crew coordination was required. Among the crew members, the bomber-radio operator (indicates enlisted man) controlled the primary bombing controls which included a Mark 15 Mod 5 bomb sight, a Mark 3 rudder control unit, the intervalometer, and

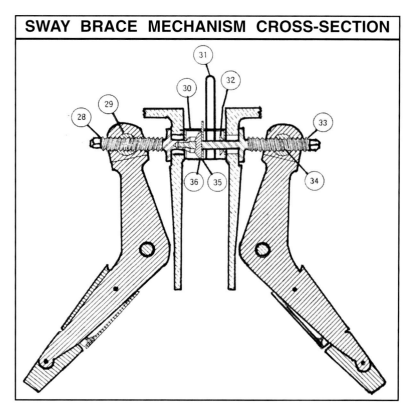

SWAY BRACE MECHANISM CROSS-SECTION

the bomb release control panel. The pilot's controls were the auxiliary bombing controls and included the master armament switch, the bomb-arming switches, and the bomb-torpedo manu-

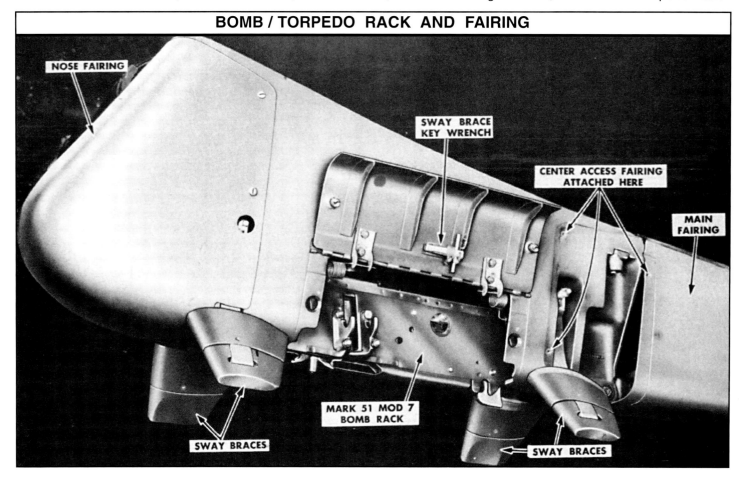

BOMB / TORPEDO RACK AND FAIRING

HOISTING 1,OOO POUND BOMB

al release. Both were provided with individual bomb selector switches, which also needed to be coordinated for proper operation. In this example of the horizontal bombing attack, the bomber would set his bomb selector switches to "SELECTIVE" for individual releases of the bombs, or,"NORMAL" if using the intervalometer to drop the bombs "in train", while the pilot selected the "NORMAL" position of his bomb-torpedo selector switches.

The S-3 Sperry autopilot used in the XTB2D-1 was a vacuum-controlled, hydraulically-powered unit that required the pilot to adjust the sensitivity of its three servo speed control valves (control knobs labeled rudder,

ARMAMENT, TWO MARK THIRTEEN TORPEDOES

ARMAMENT, TWO 2,100 POUND BOMBS

ARMAMENT, MACHINE GUNS

BORESIGHTING REFERENCE DATA

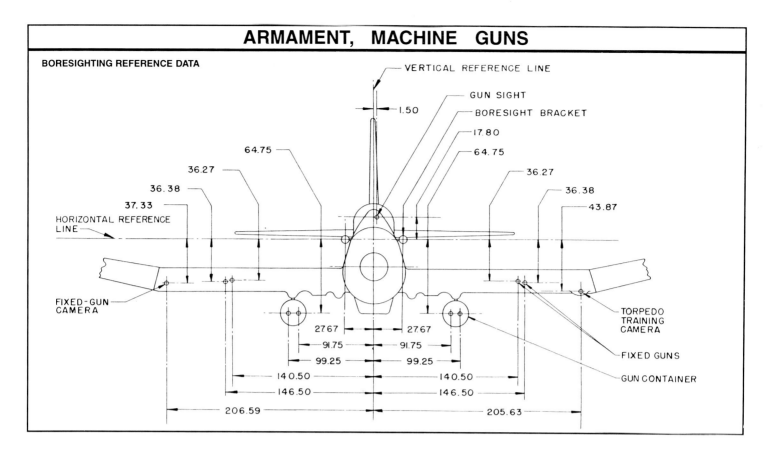

aileron, and elevator) before moving the autopilot control valve to "ENGAGE". Once the autopilot was engaged, any displacement of the rudder caused a proportional displacement of the elevator and roll-flaps as, "necessary to bank and turn the airplane smoothly". With the autopilot engaged at the start of the horizontal bomb run, the pilot transferred control of the autopilot to the bomb sight by selecting the "ON" position of the rudder control transfer valve. This enabled the bomber, through his use of the bomb sight, to control the autopilot to, "obtain precise, delicate control of the airplane and thus aid in placing the bombs upon the target". Throughout the run, the bomb sight's azimuth signals were also being sent to the PDI (Pilot Direction Indicator on the lower left of the pilot's instrument panel), where the pilot would monitor the bomb run. Although no bomb-release signal was provided, if the need arose, the pilot could use the PDI's guidance to complete the attack. If there were any problems with the electrical release, or "hung" bombs as observed by the bomber, the pilot would pull the cable-operated, bomb-torpedo manual release control handle to salvo all four wing stations simultaneously.

For its armament, the XTB2D-1 would normally be equipped with seven guns, but could be fitted with optional racks mounted at wing station 95.5. These racks would carry two MK 2 gun containers, each container equipped with two guns. All guns were Browning, basic type M-2, .50-caliber aircraft machine guns that were electrically controlled and, if they became jammed during firing, electrically recharged. The four wing guns were mounted in the center

Below, Douglas twin gun container installed on a Convair TBY-2. (National Archives)

TUNNEL GUN EQUIPMENT

wing outboard of the circle of propeller rotation. For his gun sight, the pilot used the Model RCC-4 combination sight and torpedo director. This sight was an illuminated reflector-type mounted from a brace in the windshield and could be boresighted for use as the low-altitude bomb sight. Other equipment included a gun camera and a ring and post gun sight to serve as the backup gun sight. There was no selective firing capability, so the pilot fired his guns simultaneously with the spent shells and links dropping overboard.

The gunner-inhabited Firestone model 250CH-3 turret contained two guns and was normally electrically controlled and hydraulically powered. The hydraulic system was self-contained, but had provisions for emergency manual control through two control wheels, one for elevation and the other for azimuth. The turret guns were aimed by an AN-MK 9 gun sight (the AN prefix denotes joint Army/Navy usage), an illuminated reflector-type that was mounted on a U-shaped bracket and attached to the gun elevation mechanism so that the sight and guns were simultaneously trained on a target. Other turret equipment included a gun camera, contour followers and fire-interrupters, and two containers for the spent shells and links.

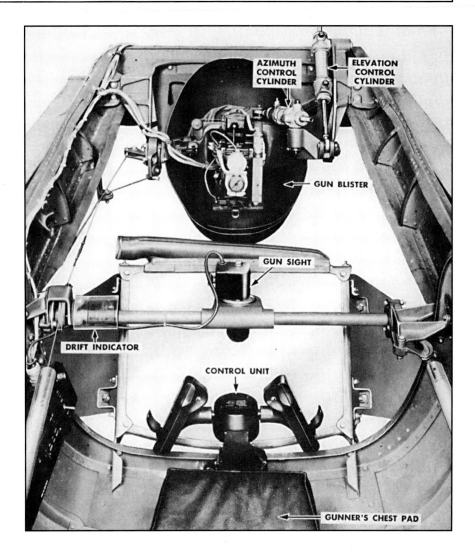

ARMAMENT INSTALLATION

The gun tunnel's flexible machine gun was mounted in a blister that was electrically controlled and hydraulically operated with fluid obtained from the main hydraulic system by a pressure-reducing valve. This tunnel gun was equipped with the MK-9 gun sight, a gun camera, and dropped its spent shells and links overboard.

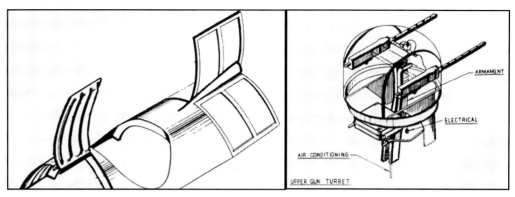

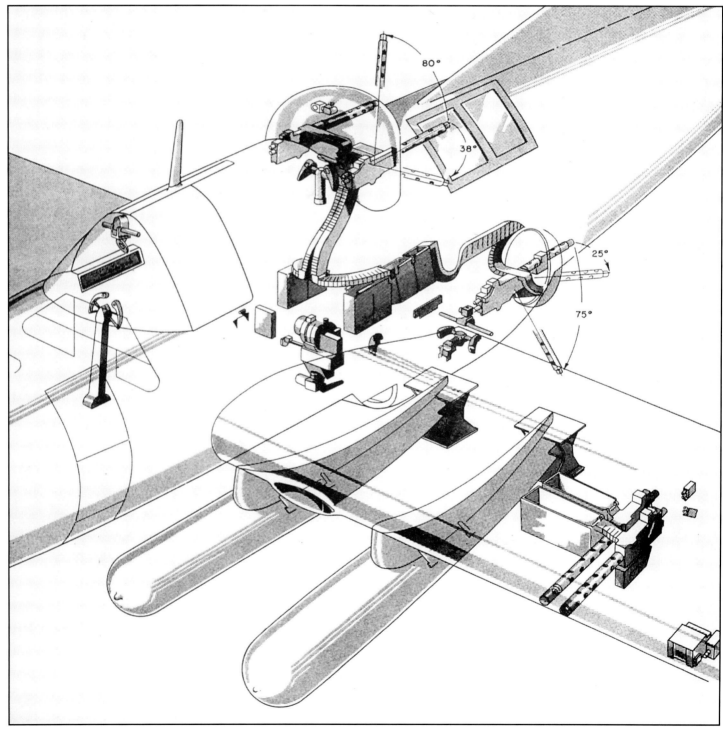

WING STORES STATIONS AND REVISED OIL COOLER SCOOP

DROPPABLE 300 GALLON WING TANKS INSTALLED ON OUTBOARD PYLONS

CONTROL SYSTEMS:

The flight control system included various tabs and devices to assure the satisfactory handling and proper control responses of the XTB2D-1. Because of that complexity, the pilot's controls differed somewhat from the stick-and-rudder airplanes of the era. The XTB2D-1 had a control wheel which provided greater mechanical advantage in controlling the aileron-type movements of the rollflaps. That function, as well as those of the elevators, rudder and trim tabs, were cable-operated (lighter and simpler than hydraulics). The large size of the control surfaces demanded that some form of "aerodynamic-boosting" be available to assist the pilot in his movements of the control surfaces. To that end, three types of tabs were employed: balance tabs, spring tabs, and trim tabs. Although each type of tab deflected in a direction opposite to the control surface's direction of deflection, their methods of operation differed. The balance tabs were connected to the underside of each outer wing panel by linkage, visible at the inboard end of the tabs, that caused the tabs to be deflected a given amount in response to a given amount of aileron-type rollflap movement. The spring tab utilized a spring within its mechanism which caused the tab's deflection to be proportional to the forces acting on the control surface, ie., the higher the force, the greater the tab's deflection. Both tabs served as boosts by reducing the forces acting on the control surface and were not adjustable in flight.

The trim tabs also served as boosts but functioned in a different manner; it was the movement of the tab that caused the aerodynamic forces to deflect the control surface. The rudder used one large combination trim and spring tab. This tab combined the rudder pedal controlled spring tab movements (10 degrees either side of neutral) with the trim tab movement (5 degrees either side of neutral) to allow a total movement of 15 degrees either side of neutral. The elevators used both trim tabs and spring tabs with the spring tabs being the inboard tabs on both elevators.

For lateral trim, the pilot's aileron trim knob acted on a "force trim" device to allow a fine adjustment of the rollflap mechanism, "trimming out" any aerodynamic forces acting on the control wheel. Thus, by using the appropriate trim tab control, the pilot was able to trim the control forces to zero for a given flight condition.

The rudder pedals could be used to either obtain the normal, independent control of the rudder or they could be interconnected to the pilot's control wheel. When interconnected, rotation of the control wheel caused a simultaneous, proportional movement of the rudder. This control-wheel-caused movement was added to the movement of the rudder pedals to increase the total rudder movement. The interconnector was designed to counteract adverse yaw, the drag caused by the downwards deflection of the up-wing rollflap, and was engaged by means of a lever on the cockpit floor.

The horizontal stabilizer was fitted with an incidence-change device to improve elevator control during landings. This device was controlled by a toggle switch that was located on the electric distribution panel and had two positions. The "NORMAL" position was one degree up from neutral (-1) while the "LANDING" position was three degrees down from neutral (+3). The "LANDING" position was incorporated to remove the nose down attitude caused by the pitching moment of full flaps, in effect increasing the down force on the elevator.

The full-span flap system, incorporated to improve the low-speed performance of the wing and satisfy its long-range cruise requirement, also replaced the conventional ailerons, landing flaps, and dive brakes. Each outboard section of the wing contained two panels of rollflaps which, along with the center wing flaps, were extended or retracted hydraulically in response to the landing flap control lever. Both the rollflaps and center wing flaps were a Douglas slotted vane type flap. When the flaps were extended, a gap was formed between them and the wing.

By extending the deflector (the vane) into that gap, a slot was created which controlled the boundary layer of air over the flap thereby increasing the value of the wing's lift coefficient. When the flaps were retracted, the concave bottom of the deflector allowed it to fit closely above the leading edge of the flaps.

The dual functions of the outer wing's rollflaps were controlled by the rollflap motion mixer, which was located above the rear spar on the floor behind the pilot's cockpit. In essence, this system consisted of a pair of narrow drums surmounted by a "massive" swinging bracket in which a smaller, wider drum was cradled. When used as ailerons, the control wheel's inputs were transmitted by cables to the smaller drum where those movements caused the larger drums to rotate, one clockwise and the other counterclockwise, pulling on opposite cables to deflect the rollflaps in opposite directions. The motion-mixer bracket did not move during these aileron-type movements. When selected by the landing flap control lever, hydraulic pressure swung the motion-mixer bracket and its cradled

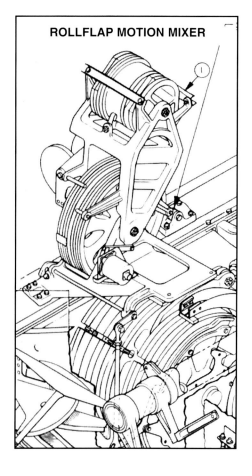

ROLLFLAP MOTION MIXER

smaller drum in an orbit-like path around the large drums. This orbit-like movement of the smaller drum pulled two cables, rotating the large drums in the same direction and deflecting both rollflaps downward. Because of the two different movements involved, rotation of the small drum for aileron-type control and orbit-like movement for landing flap control, independent and simultaneous control of the rollflaps was possible.

The amount of angular deflection allowed for the aileron-type movements of the rollflaps varied directly with their degree of downward deflection. When the rollflaps were retracted, as they would be for high speed operations, there was less aileron-type movement then when the rollflaps were extended, as for takeoffs and landings. By increasing the amount of this aileron-type movement allowed, the aerodynamic requirement of "effective control at slower speeds requires a greater range of movement of the control surface" was satisfied.

Once the rollflaps and center wing flaps were deflected to correspond to the landing flap handle's position, they were self-adjusting in their operation. This automatic adjustment of the flap deflection angle was known as "blow back", and was used to decrease excessive drag, prevent overstressing, and eliminate any adverse effect that the deflected flaps might have had on the stability and trim of the airplane.

As a synopsis, the flaps remained at the angle selected, as long as the air loads on the flaps were counterbalanced by hydraulic pressure in the load-feel valve. The air loads were determined by the airplane's airspeed, while the hydraulic pressure was determined by the position of the landing flap control lever and its subsequent setting of a leaf spring that acted on the load-feel valve. Although the airplane's weight was not a specific input, it was allowed for by the simple principle of the airplane's being heavier at take off than it would be for landing. Therefore, the lowest set of airspeed/flap values occurred when the landing flap handle was in the "LAND" position and the leaf spring was not deflected. Here, blow back would function to allow a quick reduction in excessive drag, thereby improving the wave-off characteristics of the XTB2D-1. When the landing flap handle was in "TAKE OFF", the leaf spring was partially deflected to exert an additional downward force on the load-feel valve, which then required a greater opposing hydraulic pressure before blow back would take place. The subsequent increase in the required airspeed provided the desired, greater lift coefficient during takeoff. In "ATT CONT" (the attitude control position), the leaf spring was fully deflected, exerting yet more downwards force on the load-feel valve, requiring a yet greater hydraulic pressure and so forth, until blow back, now at its highest values, would function to prevent overstressing of the flaps and wing. Finally, a load-feel relief valve was incorporated to prevent overstressing of the wing and flaps **regardless** of the landing flap control lever's position, as might occur during a dive. Blow back had retraction limits of +7 degrees and -11 degrees to ensure that the flap mechanisms were properly sequenced before their retraction was completed.

The following rollflap and center wing flap configurations were provided (retracted or extended/deflection in degrees):

CONFIGURATION	ROLLFLAP	CENTER WING FLAP
Clean	Ret./0°	Ret./0°
Landing or Takeoff	Ext./+35°	Ext./+55°
Attitude Control	Ext./+10°	Ext./+10°
Dive Brake	Ret./0°	Ext./-45°
Limits for Blow Back	Ext./+7°	Ext./-11°

Additional operational flexibility of this system allowed the pilot to select a rollflap position anywhere between "LAND" and "ATT CONT" to tailor the airplane's attitude and coefficient of lift to match the requirements of a specific mission. One such mission would have been when the XTB2D-1 was equipped the optional gun containers, and therefore armed with eight .50 caliber forward-firing machine guns, the appropriate deflection of the rollflaps would enable the airplane to fly in a nose-down attitude at moderate speeds, and "be used while the pilot is engaged in ground strafing attacks".

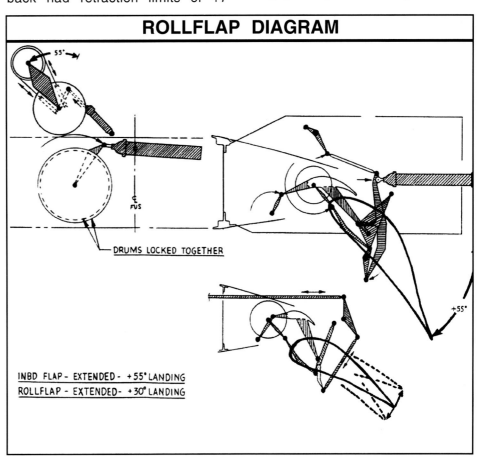

GROUND TESTING

Three views during the first engine run-up of XTB2D-1 933 at El Segundo on 2-17-45. The fairing on the fuselage under the cockpit is only located on the left hand side of the fuselage. The outer wing fairing in the bottom photo houses the rollflap hinges.

HYPOTHETICAL CARRIER-LAUNCHED MISSION

Lacking a response from the engine's manufacturer, Pratt & Whitney, I've referenced the Martin AM-1 (also powered by a R-4360) Pilot's handbook for power settings and cautionary notes for the engine. Although the engine dash models were not the same, both models were equipped with the variable speed supercharger and MAP regulator but used fuel injection carburetors from different manufacturers. The AM-1 used the CECO 100 CPB-7 carburetor for its R-4360-4W engine while the XTB2D-1's R-4360-8 was equipped with the Bendix Stromberg PR-100A3 unit.

A short review of the flap system's controls and indicator shows that the landing flap control lever was located forward of the throttle quadrant with detents marked, from forward to aft: "RETR" (retract), "NEUT" (neutral), "LAND", "TAKE OFF" and "ATT CONT". The dive brake lever was located alongside the landing flap control lever and had detents marked "RETR", "NEUT", and "DIVE", while the cruise control valve was

either "ON" or "OFF". The flap position indicator was located on the pilot's main instrument panel and showed the position of the rollflaps at all times. There were no indicators for either the center wing flaps or the dive brake.

For this mission we'll configure the XTB2D-1 per Navy specifications with two Mark 13-2 torpedoes and 302 gallons of fuel. This configuration had a "useful load" (Navy terminology that includes the crew, fuel ordnance, etc.) of 8,504 lbs and a takeoff gross weight of 26,343 lbs. The standard operating procedure for takeoff of single-engine airplanes during carrier operations called for the use of full flaps and military power. These were set by positioning the landing flap control lever to "TAKEOFF" (roll flaps 35 degrees and center wing flaps 55 degrees) and the powerplant controls to 53" MAP and 2,700 RPM. The military power rating of 3,000 BHP had a 5 minute time limit and was based on the use of 100/130 octane AvGas. With the use of the soon-to-be-developed 115/145 AvGas and its improved detonation characteristics, the engine's power rating could have been increased. Using the standard wind-over-the-deck of 25 knots, the take-off distance for our configuration was estimated to be 430 feet.

Once airborne, and as its airspeed increased, blow back would start to incrementally retract both sets of flaps, reducing excessive drag

Above and below, 3/4 rear view showing temporary turtledeck fairing over proposed gun turret position.

Above, note the large carburetor airscoop on top of the fuselage.

while maintaining adequate lift, until its limit of seven degrees deflection was reached. Once the airspeed was fast enough to allow the pilot to fully retract the flaps, he would select "RETR" (all flaps retracted & faired) to obtain the clean wing for high speed operation. After the wing flap indicator showed that the rollflaps were faired, the landing flap control lever would be positioned to "NEUT", reducing the amount of hydraulic line under pressure to lessen the possibility of line failure.

Also during this "clean up" phase of the flight, adherence to military power's time limit required a power reduction. We'll reduce power to 43.5" MAP and 2,550 RPM, the normal rated power settings, developing 2,450 BHP at 2,000 ft. with no time limit. (In actual practice, the flight leader would use slightly less power, perhaps 40" MAP and 2,400 RPM, which allowed the other pilots the use of that difference, before they were in danger of exceeding normal rated power limits). After MAP and RPM were set, the mixture control would be placed to "NORMAL" and the airspeed increased to help cool the R-4360 while climbing to rendezvous. At this low altitude, 43.5" MAP was attained at less than the full throttle position, but as the climb-out continued the throttle needed be advanced to maintain the 43.5" MAP. Around 5,000 ft, which varied according to the efficiency of the individual engine, the full throttle position would be reached and the supercharger's impeller would start increasing its speed to maintain MAP. In this variable speed range of the supercharger, if a wingman needed to add power to maintain formation, attention to droop caused him to modify his normal smooth, incremental throttle movements; "the time lag during variable speed operation may be shortened by moving the throttle **full forward** and as the manifold pressure starts to increase, retard it to the position that will maintain the desired manifold pressure." By 13,500 ft, the supercharger's impeller would be in full high ratio (7.52:1) and the engine would be developing 2,400 BHP. The throttle was now full forward and MAP would continue to decrease as the altitude increased so that at our cruise altitude of 19,000 ft, the normal rated power settings would be 38" MAP and 2,550 RPM to produce 2,100 BHP.

After leveling off and accelerating to 155 kts IAS (Indicated Air Speed), the procedures required to configure the wing for LRC (Long Range Cruise) included cruise control valve to "CRUISE" and the landing flap control lever to "ATT CONT" (all flaps remained retracted but now deflected 10 degrees downward). The resulting change in the camber of the wing was incorporated to increase range, while blow back protection was provided to prevent overstressing of the flaps or wing. At 19,000 ft and an OAT (Outside Air Temperature) of 0 degrees Fahrenheit (Standard +9), the IAS of 155 kts works out to a TAS (True Air Speed) of about 215 kts (248 mph for the readers who like bigger numbers). The airplane's weight, lighter now by the weight of the fuel burned-off, would be approximately 25,000 lbs. Based on the Flight Operation Instruction Charts for a 25,000 lb Mauler, we'll set 33" MAP and 2,400 RPM which should produce 1,625 BHP as our cruise power. Since the 33" MAP was the allowable maximum for that combination of RPM and altitude, if a wingman needed more power he had to increase the engine's RPM first, to allow for an increase in MAP, or be in danger of "overboosting" his engine.

Anytime the need arose, such as encountering clouds that caused the loss of visual flight reference, the pilot could use the autopilot's vacuum-powered gyro instruments as aids in determining the airplane's attitude and heading. These instruments, the bank-and-climb gyro and the directional gyro, were incorporated as guidance controls for the autopilot servos and were operated by an engine-driven vacuum pump. Once the instruments were "uncaged" for use, normally done prior to take off, the bank-and-climb gyro and its artificial horizon bar could be used to improve the pilot's "blind-flying" instrument scan of "needle, ball and

airspeed".

To prepare for combat, approaching the target area the landing flap control lever would first be moved to "RETR" and the cruise control valve to "OFF" (all flaps retracted and fared), restoring the clean wing for high speed operations. Then the landing flap control lever would be placed in "NEUT" in anticipation of the use of dive flaps. The bomber-radio operator would descend into the gun tunnel to set his bomb selector switches to "NORMAL", the intervalometer switch to "BYPASS", and transfer the bomb release switch plug to the dummy receptacle before manning the aft-facing flexible machine gun. Once the bomber's switches were properly set the pilot would complete the torpedo release electrical circuit by positioning the torpedo selector switches to "SELECT" and the master armament switch to "ON". To initiate his attack, the pilot would place the mixture control to "AUTO RICH", reduce MAP to between 15" and 20", prop pitch to 2,300 RPM, the dive flap control lever to "DIVE" (roll flaps retracted and fared, center wing flaps extended and deflected 45 degrees upwards) then to "NEUT" after starting a 50 degree dive. The specifications had required that the dive brake increase drag, "with a negligible effect on attitude of the airplane and the stick force required for trim", and also that "Special precautions shall be taken to locate the horizontal tail surface above the dive brake wake." The dive brake had a limiting airspeed of 425mph (368 kts) IAS, above which blow back functioned through the previously described load-feel relief valve to prevent over-stressing of the dive brake flap panels

Above, unusual head-on view of the XTB2D-1 with the propellers out of sync. The forward row of prop blades was smaller by inches.

Below, 2-26-45 side view shows temporary turtledeck cover for twin gun turret which was never supplied by the government.

of the wing. That high a limiting airspeed indicates that the role of the dive brake was to enable the XTB2D-1 to reach its torpedo/ attack altitude as quickly as possible. This differed from the dive-bombing attack, where the dive brakes' role was to maintain a moderate speed, and thereby allow more time for the pilot to correct his aim. The throttle setting for the dive was based on two factors: using enough power to maintain the dive speed without triggering blow back, and on the need to "keep the engine a little warm and to burn away any oil that may pass the piston rings". Similarly, the RPM was set at 2,300 to help avoid overspeeding the propeller. At the start of the pull-out, the pilot needed to position the dive brake to "RETR" and then "open the throttle very slowly at completion of dive so partly cooled engine will not cut out". The torpedo attack was probably made from the Navy's seemingly-standard 400 feet and at an airspeed that can be inferred from: "the torpedo shall be so installed that its launching attitude is between horizontal and 3 degrees nose up when the airplane is flying at a speed of 225mph (195kts) at sea level". The pilot would use the control wheel's "pickle-switch" to drop the torpedoes and, if any failed to release, pull the manual release control handle to salvo them.

In anticipation of the carrier landing, but before entering the "Charlie" pattern, the pilot would drop the arresting hook and, after centering the rudder pedals and control wheel, his right hand could reach down to pull the rudder-rollflap interconnector engagement lever up. The additional rudder movement thus gained would be most useful now, in this low-speed flight regime of carrier landings. At the break, the pilot's left hand would push the prop pitch to "INCREASE RPM", mixture control forward to "AUTO RICH", throttle back to 15" MAP, place the landing gear lever "DOWN", the landing flap control lever to "LAND" (all flaps would extend, rollflaps deflected 35 degrees, center wing flaps 55 degrees) before moving onto the control wheel. His right hand was then free to toggle the stabilizer

position switch to "LANDING", helping to avoid a nose-wheel first touchdown with its dire consequences.

Thanks to the large flap area (18.9% of total wing area) of this full-span flap system, the XTB2D-1 pilot would have been able to fly his carrier pass at the contemporary carrier pattern speeds. The pilot would start his landing pattern turn "at the one-eighty" and, because of the increase in stall speed caused by the bank angle, fly at an airspeed that was slightly faster (5-10 kts) then it would be when the wings were leveled approaching the "cut". Based on normal practice, the LSO would expect the pilot to be set-up (on altitude and power) at the "ninety", then work on alignment while planning on a short straight-in for the speed reduction which "wings level" would allow. The XTB2D-1 did provide the pilot with "good" over-the-nose visibility to accommodate this final, where the pilot could slow to "cut" speed and blow back would allow the flaps to be fully deflected.

If given a "wave-off", blow back protection was set to reduce excessive drag and improve the wave off characteristics of the XTB2D-1. But as the pilot started to bank into his clearing turn, which would be steeper then the landing pattern's turn, the airplane's stall speed would be increased. To allow sharp turns at these slow speeds, the designers included a "maneuver flap" function which utilized the centrifugal forces created by the turn for its control. The centrifugal force acted on an inert weight to upset the equilibrium that existed in the load-feel valve thereby allowing a greater downward flap deflection for that airspeed. When the bank angle decreased, the centrifugal force decreased and allowed the force of the airloads on the load-feel valve to blow back the flaps proportionately. All these changes of the flap deflection angle were achieved through the "LAND" position of the landing flap control lever and without any direct input from the pilot. Although this flight control system was complex, for the pilot its operation was simple and can be viewed as a forerunner to today's computer-controlled flight systems.

For an insight into what the XTB2D-1 might have offered the Fleet, the following information, taken from the Douglas Aircraft Company report entitled "Analysis of the Tactical Usefulness of the model XTB2D-1 Airplane", dated December 1944, is offered: "This Torpedo Bomber will carry two torpedoes or 2,000 pound bombs off an Essex class flight deck; or four torpedoes or 2,000 pound bombs from an airstrip. Tiny Tims with lanyard may be carried in place of other loadings. The alternate use of this airplane as a long-

Above, rare inflight photo of the Skypirate on 5-9-45. The aircraft is landing at El Segundo with the flaps extended.

range scout with radar search makes it especially adapted for CV and CVB type carriers".

"In addition to the ability of the XTB2D-1 to combine these loadings and take-offs, this airplane is capable of very long-range bombings. With speeds approaching those of the fastest attack bombers, the XTB2D-1 is well fitted for present day operation and is the most effective weapon now available for blasting Japan's coastal shipping".

Also, the following comparison of the contemporary torpedo bombers was included in the report. Fort this comparison, each airplane was similarly configured: full internal fuel, one 300 gallon droppable fuel tank, one torpedo for the Combat mission and without the torpedo for the Scout mission.

MISSION RADIUS NAUTICAL MILES

AIRCRAFT	COMBAT	SCOUT
TBF/TBM	420	640
TBY	500	751
XTB2D-1	850	795

Combat Radius: One-half the cruising distance with an allowance for 20 min. for rendezvous, 15 min. at combat and 60 min. fuel reserve. Tanks dropped at target.

Scouting Radius: One-third of cruising distance at speed for max range at 1,500 ft. allowing a 60 min. fuel reserve. Tanks are retained.

Among its contemporaries, the XTB2D-1 was the fastest, had the greatest range, and was further set apart by its unmatched capability to carry two torpedoes which, with a fuel load of full internal fuel plus two 300 gallon drop tanks, offered a Combat Radius of 1,000 nm. Or, if loaded with full internal fuel and four 300 gallon drop tanks, a Scouting Radius of 1,328 nm was predicted. But, by 1944 the potential promised by the single-place, multi-mission XBT designs

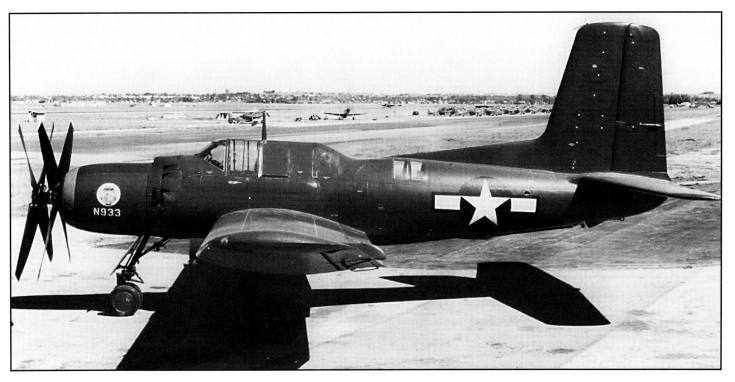

Above, 36933 on a early test flight in clean flight condition sans spinner.

then under development, served to eclipse any benefits that the XTB2D-1 would have offered.

By the time the XTB2D-1 first flew in 1945, the end of the design as a combat airplane was a foregone conclusion. Because of that and their status as experimental airplanes, the two airplanes differed from the specification's design in several aspects the most obvious difference being the deletion of the turret and gun tunnel which drastically altered the "look" of the design. While each prototype treated the "fared over" gun tunnel in the same manner, each was equipped with its distinctive dorsal faring. These farings were made of sheet aluminum and attached to the fuselage in the same manner as the turret and gun tunnel would have been. This method of attachment, along with the 1943 requirement that the gun tunnel be a "separate, detachable assembly", and "be considered as an alternate installation", makes one suspicious and wonder if BuAer had missions other than those called for in the specifications planned for the airplane. Although the 1943 specifications called for "just the first airplane to be completed without the turret and gun tunnel", the fact that the second airplane also omitted that defensive armament could indicate that a change in mission requirements occurred significantly before BuNo 36934 was completed. The next noteworthy difference is in the length of the vertical stabilizer on each prototype. BuNo 36933 was equipped with a 10'6" long vertical stabilizer which resulted in a "Height over Tail" dimension of 18'6". BuNo 36934 was constructed with a stabilizer that was shorter, more rectangular in planform, and had a "Height over Tail" dimension of 16'7". Since this was the same "Height over Tail" dimension as other tricycle landing gear, carrier-based airplanes, the Grumman F7F and S2F as examples, one is lead to believe that this dimension was a limitation based on the physical constraints of the hangar deck. Up to now, no aerodynamic reason for this change has surfaced, so regardless of whether the aforementioned reason is correct or not, the shorter vertical stabilizer would have increased the XTB2D-1's carrier-suitability.

To summarize, we have three dis-

At left, shortened 8'7" vertical stabilizer as used on the second XTB2D-1 (BuNo 36934)

tinctive fuselage shapes for the XTB2D-1. The first, designed to meet the 1943 specifications, included the turret, tunnel gun, and the longer vertical stabilizer. When constructed, BuNo 36933 omitted the gun tunnel, substituted a decidedly-angular dorsal fairing for the turret but kept the longer stabilizer. BuNo 36934 was also without the defensive armament, featuring instead the streamlined turtledeck and its shorter, broader-looking vertical stabilizer in what might have been the standard for a limited production run.

In addition to the two prototypes, the Navy had contracted for 23 additional Skypirates, BuNos 89097-89119. This small number of airplanes would indicate that the Navy was planning to equip one squadron which would train and deploy detachments aboard Midway class carriers, which in 1944 had six hulls (CVBs 41-44 and 56-57) planned for construction. In the end, none of the airplanes from this second block of BuNos, or any of the last three CVBs, were produced.

The aircraft never flew with the spinner installed, nor were many photos taken with the spinner installed on the ground. Most published photos of the spinner installation are photos that have had the spinner airbrushed in. Either the propeller's operating mechanism required too much on-going attention to warrant installing the spinner, or the spinner's design

At right, the short-tailed second prototype (36934) in flight. The engine cowl ring was red.

wasn't meeting the cooling needs of the four-row R-4360.

For the flight test phase of their development, both prototypes were equipped with a cable-operated spin chute located in the tail cone, and fire detection and extinguishing systems. Specific flight test instrumentation included an accelerometer, Vg recorder, torque-meter, fuel flow-meter, oil outlet temperature indicator, and a carburetor air temperature indicator. At one time during its development, BuNo 36933 was equipped with the Firestone turret, its guns and control panel, the bomber's radio-electric-oxygen panel, the bomb release control panel and junction box, the tunnel gun and its control panel, and provision for a fixed mapping camera, Fairchild K17 F56 either 8.25 or 20 inch installation. The location of the camera installation was the same as the forward part of the gun tunnel, between fuselage stations 129 and 144.5.

The 1943 specifications had stated, "No provisions shall be made on experimental airplanes to provide angular fin adjustment". This refers to the horizontal stabilizer incidence-change device designed to counter the nose down attitude caused by full flaps. The need for the horizontal stabilizer incidence-change device ended in 1944 with the design of the Douglas XBT2D-1 Skyraider and its adjustable horizontal stabilizer. That electrically operated device offered the pilot the capability of selecting a fine degree of trim throughout the range of six degrees nose up to four degrees nose down, effectively rendering the Skypirate's two-position system obsolete.

There also were two requirements that have not appeared in any

At right, the second prototype (36934) shows off the clean aerodynamic turtledeck fairing over the proposed turret position.

of the photographs: a partial-span flap system, designed as an alternative to the full-span flap system, and the heat anti-icing system. In this partial-span flap system, the outermost rollflap was an aileron while the inner panel a wing flap, to be used only as a high-lift device. As a means of identifying either flap system, the partial-span's aileron used two tabs, the outer being the spring tab while the inboard was the trim tab. The blowback feature of the full-span flap system was retained for the dive brake, take off, and landing operations, which implies that the attitude control function of the full-span system was not part of this partial-span flap system.

The heat anti-icing system utilized heated air to anti-ice the outer wing panels and tail surfaces while providing limited de-icing for the center wing. The heaters for this system were located in the leading edges of the center wing outboard of the oil cooler ducts, and at the base of the vertical fin, and used fuel supplied from the main fuel tank for their combustion. The air supply for either anti-icing or the heater's combustion entered through small ducts located in the outboard portion of the oil cooler ducts and in the fairing at the base of the vertical fin. The system was designed to anti-ice the forward 12% of selected airfoil's chord by routing the heated air along the nose section of the appropriate airfoil to its tip, then across the airfoil to exhaust ahead of the attached control surfaces. As a way to lighten the pilot's workload, once selected by a lever located behind the pilot's left elbow, control would be automatic, eliminating the need for temperature indicators and selector switches. As can be seen in the photographs, the air inlet duct in the vertical fin was not incorporated, from which the assumption can be made that, even if the heater was installed, it wasn't intended to be operational.

The scarcity of in-flight photos, and the lack of any reference indicating that the XTB2D-1 was accepted by the Navy, points out how limited its flight test program must have been. Although the concept of the XTB2D-1 was obsolete by war's end, the mid-war requirement for a long-range first-strike torpedo bomber had to be responded to. The creativity demonstrated by its designers in developing the design to its high level of performance cannot be denied. That the Douglas design team, headed by Ed Heinemann with Bob Donovan as chief engineer, was able to fulfill the Navy's demanding requirements is yet another credit to their genius and discipline.

The following table was compiled from "Detail Specification for Model XTB2D-1 Airplane Class VTB", issued in 1943 and useing weights that were estimated pending completion of the first XTB2D-1. Also, in compiling the data into table form some contradictions in the term "Useful load" arose. With that in mind, the following is offered:

At right, the end of the line, the second XTB2D-1 BuNo 36934 is hoisted aboard a barge on 3-12-48. The intended destination of the aircraft is believed to be Terminal Island. Final disposition of the two XTB2D-1s is not known.

XTB2D-1 MISSION	TORPEDO BOMBER	HORIZONTAL BOMBER	OVERLOAD SCOUT
Specification paragraph:	104B	104H	104L
Crew (3)	600 lbs	600 lbs	600 lbs
Fuel Quantity	320 gal	501 gal	1,074 gal
fuselage tank	320 gal	501 gal	501 gal
wing tanks	N/A	N/A	273 gal
droppable tank (300 gal)	N/A	N/A	300 gal
Fuel Weight (6lbs per gal includes 20 lbs trapped in system)	1,940 lbs	3,026 lbs	6,762 lbs
Weight of integral wing tanks	N/A	N/A	350 lbs
Weight of droppable tank, structure, rack etc.	N/A	N/A	298 lbs
Engine oil	18 gal	28 gal	60 gal
Oil weight (7.5 lbs per gal includes 90 lbs trapped in system)	225 lbs	300 lbs	540 lbs
Armament (includes installation)			
2 fixed guns, ammunition, etc.	285 lbs	285 lbs	285 lbs
RCC-4 torpedo director	26 lbs	o lbs	0 lbs
3 flexible guns, etc.	576 lbs	576 lbs	576 lbs
Equipment (includes radios, radar, oxygen, life rafts, etc.)	414 lbs	414 lbs	414 lbs
Torpedoes, 2 Mk 13-2 plus installation	4,464 lbs	N/A	N/A
Armor piercing bombs, 2 1,600 lb plus installation	N/A	3,422 lbs	N/A
Useful Load:	8,504 lbs	8,323 lbs	9,527 lbs
XTB2D-1 empty weight; airframe, engine, fixed equipment etc. as per paragraph 105A	17,839 lbs	17,839 lbs	17,839 lbs
Empty weight balance 27 % M.A.C. XTB2D-1 Gross weight as per paragraph 102A	26,343 lbs	26,462 lbs	27,366 lbs

PILOT'S COCKPIT ARRANGEMENT

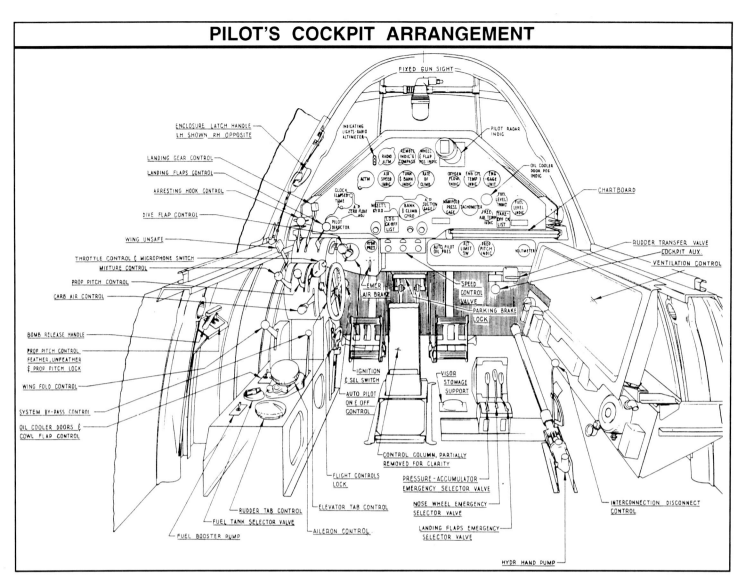

RIGHT HAND PILOT'S CONSOLE

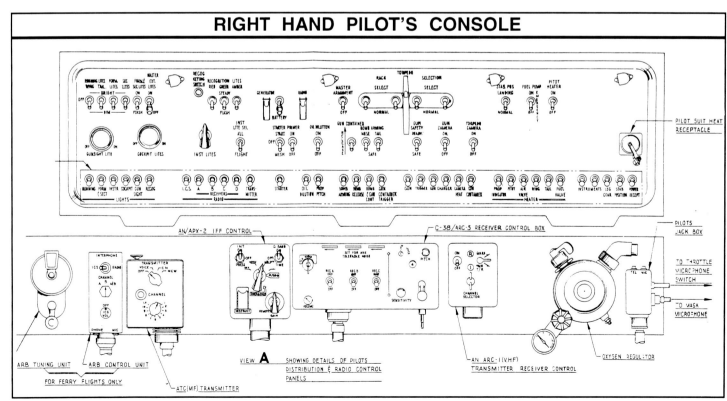

CONTROL WHEEL SWITCHES

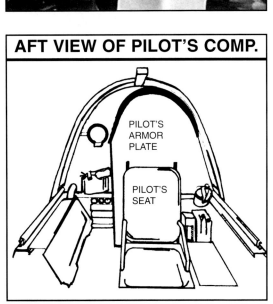

AFT VIEW OF PILOT'S COMP.

BOMB RELEASE PANEL

PILOT'S INSTRUMENT PANEL

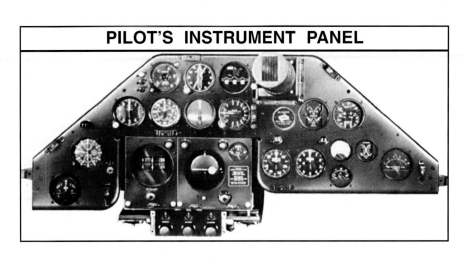

PILOT'S RIGHT HAND CONSOLE

LEFT HAND PILOT'S CONSOLE

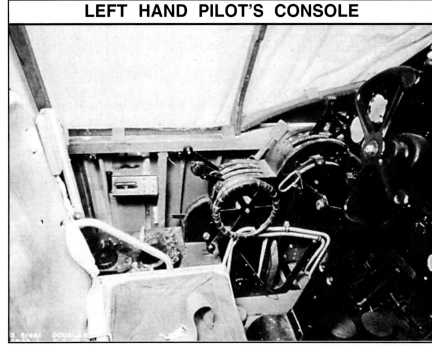

HYDRAULIC EMERGENCY CONTROL PEDESTAL AND HAND PUMP

RADIO AFTER COMPARTMENT

ELECTRONIC EQUIPMENT

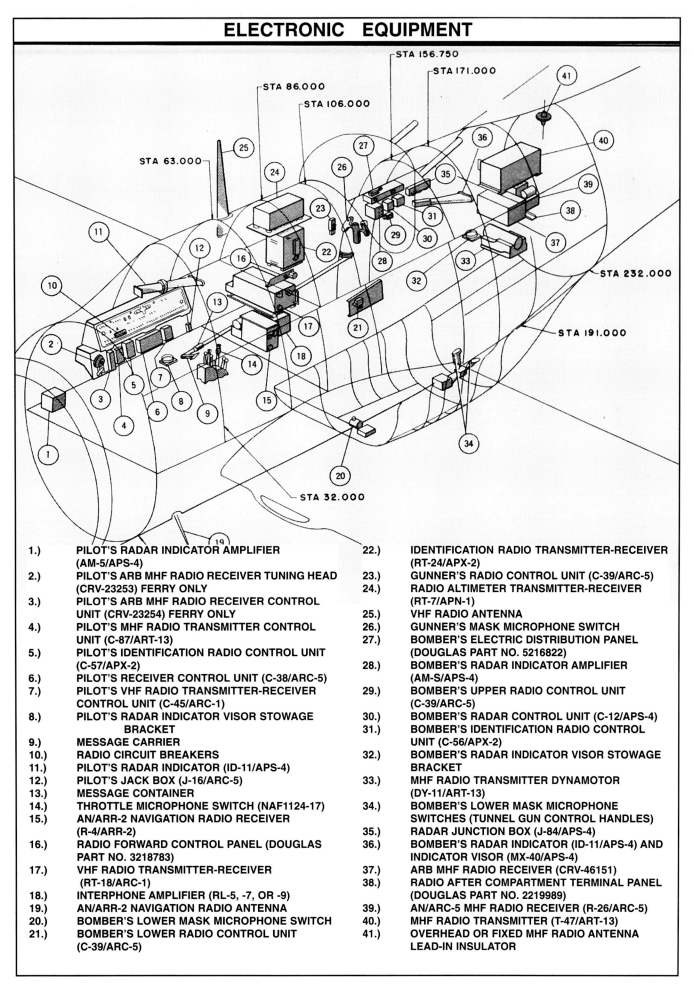

1.) PILOT'S RADAR INDICATOR AMPLIFIER (AM-5/APS-4)
2.) PILOT'S ARB MHF RADIO RECEIVER TUNING HEAD (CRV-23253) FERRY ONLY
3.) PILOT'S ARB MHF RADIO RECEIVER CONTROL UNIT (CRV-23254) FERRY ONLY
4.) PILOT'S MHF RADIO TRANSMITTER CONTROL UNIT (C-87/ART-13)
5.) PILOT'S IDENTIFICATION RADIO CONTROL UNIT (C-57/APX-2)
6.) PILOT'S RECEIVER CONTROL UNIT (C-38/ARC-5)
7.) PILOT'S VHF RADIO TRANSMITTER-RECEIVER CONTROL UNIT (C-45/ARC-1)
8.) PILOT'S RADAR INDICATOR VISOR STOWAGE BRACKET
9.) MESSAGE CARRIER
10.) RADIO CIRCUIT BREAKERS
11.) PILOT'S RADAR INDICATOR (ID-11/APS-4)
12.) PILOT'S JACK BOX (J-16/ARC-5)
13.) MESSAGE CONTAINER
14.) THROTTLE MICROPHONE SWITCH (NAF1124-17)
15.) AN/ARR-2 NAVIGATION RADIO RECEIVER (R-4/ARR-2)
16.) RADIO FORWARD CONTROL PANEL (DOUGLAS PART NO. 3218783)
17.) VHF RADIO TRANSMITTER-RECEIVER (RT-18/ARC-1)
18.) INTERPHONE AMPLIFIER (RL-5, -7, OR -9)
19.) AN/ARR-2 NAVIGATION RADIO ANTENNA
20.) BOMBER'S LOWER MASK MICROPHONE SWITCH
21.) BOMBER'S LOWER RADIO CONTROL UNIT (C-39/ARC-5)
22.) IDENTIFICATION RADIO TRANSMITTER-RECEIVER (RT-24/APX-2)
23.) GUNNER'S RADIO CONTROL UNIT (C-39/ARC-5)
24.) RADIO ALTIMETER TRANSMITTER-RECEIVER (RT-7/APN-1)
25.) VHF RADIO ANTENNA
26.) GUNNER'S MASK MICROPHONE SWITCH
27.) BOMBER'S ELECTRIC DISTRIBUTION PANEL (DOUGLAS PART NO. 5216822)
28.) BOMBER'S RADAR INDICATOR AMPLIFIER (AM-S/APS-4)
29.) BOMBER'S UPPER RADIO CONTROL UNIT (C-39/ARC-5)
30.) BOMBER'S RADAR CONTROL UNIT (C-12/APS-4)
31.) BOMBER'S IDENTIFICATION RADIO CONTROL UNIT (C-56/APX-2)
32.) BOMBER'S RADAR INDICATOR VISOR STOWAGE BRACKET
33.) MHF RADIO TRANSMITTER DYNAMOTOR (DY-11/ART-13)
34.) BOMBER'S LOWER MASK MICROPHONE SWITCHES (TUNNEL GUN CONTROL HANDLES)
35.) RADAR JUNCTION BOX (J-84/APS-4)
36.) BOMBER'S RADAR INDICATOR (ID-11/APS-4) AND INDICATOR VISOR (MX-40/APS-4)
37.) ARB MHF RADIO RECEIVER (CRV-46151)
38.) RADIO AFTER COMPARTMENT TERMINAL PANEL (DOUGLAS PART NO. 2219989)
39.) AN/ARC-5 MHF RADIO RECEIVER (R-26/ARC-5)
40.) MHF RADIO TRANSMITTER (T-47/ART-13)
41.) OVERHEAD OR FIXED MHF RADIO ANTENNA LEAD-IN INSULATOR

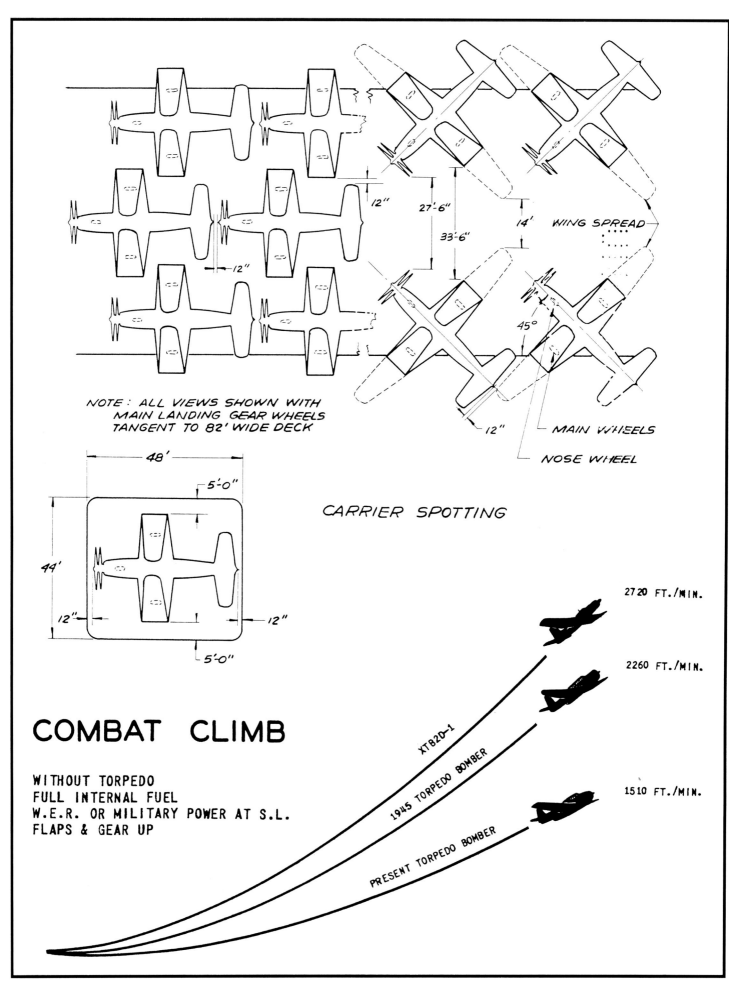